Sit Tim!

Written by Jan Burchett
and Sara Vogler
Illustrated by Roman Diaz

Collins

tap tap tap

2

pad pad pad

3

a map

5

Tim naps.

Sam tips a tin!

10

Dad tips it in.

Tim tips it! Tim sips.

Dad sips. Sam sips.

14

15

🐾 Review: After reading 🐾

Use your assessment from hearing the children read to choose any GPCs and words that need additional practice.

Read 1: Decoding

- Point to and read **map** on page 5. Ask: What sort of things does a map show? (e.g. *streets, buildings, paths*) Why might Sam need a map? (e.g. *so they know where to go in the park*)
- Point to **Tim** on page 7, allowing the children to sound and blend out loud. Repeat for **tin**. Then turn to pages 8 and 9 and encourage the children to blend in their heads, silently, before reading the words aloud.
- Look at the "I spy sounds" pages (14–15) together. Ask the children to point out as many things as they can in the picture that begin with the /m/ sound. (*mug, muffin, map, mouse, mums, menu, man, mop, motorbike*)

Read 2: Prosody

- Focus on how to use a storyteller voice, using a change of tone when something dramatic happens.
  - o On page 8, encourage the children to read the words quietly because Tim is napping.
  - o On page 9, say: Something has happened, so can you read these words with surprise?
  - o Ask the children to read both pages, using a storyteller's changing tone to draw the listener in.

Read 3: Comprehension

- Talk about any dogs the children have experienced or seen. What do they like best about Tim?
- Ask the children:
  - o On page 2, what makes the tapping noise? (*Dad's cane*) Why do you think he has a cane? (e.g. *Dad cannot see very well and uses his cane to find things in front of him*)
  - o On page 11, what does Dad tip in the tin? (*water*) Why? (e.g. *so Tim can drink it*)
- Discuss what other tricks Tim might be taught, as well as **Sit**. (e.g. *wait, lie down, come*) Talk about why people teach dogs to sit down or keep still. (e.g. *so the dog doesn't run away*)